Contributors

Roxanne Rhoads: Bewitching Book Tours
Zachary Hagen: A Writing Process that Works: Being a Neurodivergent Author
Charles Porter: Confessions of a writer?
Rod A. Walters: Sex sells
Kathy Martone: GOLD STAR CONFESSIONS
Celinka Serre: I Rarely Write in Consecutive Order
Brett Atlas: Three Things Matter Most: Linking Time, Relationships, and Money
Angela Page and Mia Altieri: There's a Dead Girl In My Yard
Charles Porter: Shallcross
Brett Bloemendaal: Fishing for More
Jonathan Koven: Below Torrential Hill
VK Tritschler: Good Enough
Kaleb Quist: The Golden Age of Oversaturation
Michael J. Brooks: Lessons Learned from the Bumps, Bruises, and Trials of Publishing
Maxwell F. Hurley: It's Not a Good Fit for Us
Donald Furrow-Scott: Whom are You Writing For?
Tosca Lee: The Line Between
Susanna Allen: That Magic Mischief
Jennifer Allis Provost: Oleander
Mercedes R. Lackey: The Silver Bullets of Annie Oakley
Neil Perry Gordon: Otzi's Odyssey
Dave Mainelli: How To Be Lonely
Brett Salter: The Search for Synergy
Brian Terenna: The Astral Hacker
Felicia Wartson: The Risks of Dead Reckoning
Kristian Hägglund: You Are Special

Photo Credits from Pexels:
Ashutosh-Sonwani p.2
Stanislav-Kondratiev p.13
Nida p.19
Saliha p.30
Wallace-Chuck p.34-43

Special thanks to:
Christopher R. Main

COPYRIGHT © 2022
Review Tales Magazine
A Book Magazine for Indie Authors
This magazine may not be reproduced, either in part or in its entirety, in any form, by any means, without written permission from the publisher, with the exception of brief excerpts for purposes of radio, television, or published review. Although all possible means have been taken to ensure the accuracy of the material presented, Review Tales is not liable for any misinterpretation, misapplication or typographical errors.
All rights, including the right of translation, are reserved.
Founder & Editor in Chief: S. Jeyran Main
Publisher: Review Tales Publishing & Editing Services
Print & distribution: Ingram Spark
Cover Photo: Olya-Kobruseva
Designs: Pexels
ISBN 978-1-988680-14-9 (paperback)
ISBN 978-1-988680-15-6 (digital)
www.jeyranmain.com
For all inquiries please contact us directly.

Contents

01 Editor's Note

02 Author Confessions

13 Book Reviews

19 Words of Wisdom

30 Author Interview

41 Starred Books

Editor's Note

There is something special about spring that encourages everyone to look forward, set their clocks ahead, and not look back at the past season. Here we are with the second issue bringing you so much hope and optimism.

Lately, I've been communicating with authors and hearing their frustrations. It isn't easy, and I see how much they want to succeed in this process. But as hard as they work, as many times as they find the courage to get back on the drawing board, I say, keep at it and keep trying.

The truth is, we are doing good! There is no need to justify it. No matter how many revisions and setbacks we encounter, we need to remember that the writing life is messy. There is no secret to success. Instead, we find many paths leading us to where we want to go, and if we keep trying, we will get there.

This issue offers some raw confessions and vulnerable discussions that you will enjoy. You will realize that you aren't alone and how relatable your struggles are with your fellow writers. Let's enjoy what we have and aim for better things.

Jeyran Main

Founder & Editor-in-chief
Review Tales Magazine - Publishing & Editing Services

AUTHOR

Confessions

Contributors:
Zachary Hagen
Charles Porter
Rod A. Walters
Kathy Martone
Celinka Serre

JEYRANMAIN.COM

ETERNITY'S MIRROR

Zachary Hagen

Publication Date: March 22, 2022
ISBN: 978-1-737190-96-7
Book Category/Genre: New/Young Adult Fantasy
Page Count: 322
Publisher: First Horizons Publishing

A Writing Process that Works: Being a Neurodivergent Author

Written by Zachary Hagen

ADHD is either a curse or a superpower. It oscillates from day to day, and there are no in-betweens. This is a life of extremes for me and others like me. So how do we do something that requires such intense focus for sustained periods? After all, it takes months to complete a book for most people, perhaps longer.
I can't say how other neurodivergent people accomplish this, but I can tell you how I do it.

Zachary Hagen is a Minnesota-based fantasy author and editor. He lives there with his wife, Claudia, and their dog, Flynn. When he isn't busy writing his next book or working with an editing client, you can often find him walking around his neighborhood or hiking.

First off, I have to have a plan. The fact is, if I don't have a set plan, spontaneity dictates that I either watch Netflix or read all day, so I cannot wait to be inspired. I can't wait for the story to tell itself to me as I write. I have to plot it out. I look at who my main character is, their goals, what problems they'll face, and how I want the book to end. Then I work through the story's structure with act summaries, one-line chapter prompts with the plot point I'm covering there, and I end with full chapter summaries. If you have ever read Plot & Structure by James Scott Bell, you might recognize that as The Borg Outline (166-170).

Then, as many other neurodivergent people will tell you, routine is everything. I finished my first two books and am making headway on the third because of routine. I have set times when I sit down and write and work on things to further my career as an author. I make the time, and it works for me.

So, if you're neurodivergent and want to write or accomplish anything, here is how I would suggest going about it. Take advantage of the initial spark of inspiration and create a plan. Don't' start on the meat of the project, or it will lose momentum and never see the light of day. Use that plan to establish a routine and work a little towards it daily. Then, celebrate your success once the project is done and repeat it.

BLINDSPOT CATHEDRAL

Charles Porter

Publication Date: 2014
ISBN: 978-0-989425-60-5
Book Category/Genre: Fiction
Page Count: 244
Publisher: Independent

Confessions of a Writer?

Written by Charles Porter

Confessions of a writer? I was once a practicing Catholic. When I was eight years old, the nuns would make me go to confession. I was so innocent I had to make up the sins, and they were all venial sins—I didn't know how to commit a mortal sin. I probably got nine out of the Ten Commandments broke in the years that came, everything but murder, and I thought some people deserved that. I am seventy-eight now. When I was twelve years old, someone turned a radio on in my head and never came back to turn it off.

Born in 1944, Charles Porter grew up in Stuart, Florida, on the St. Lucie River in the same old wooden house where his father was born. His first novel in the Hearing Voices series, Shallcross: The Blindspot Cathedral, won Kirkus Reviews Best Books of 2014 award. In 2017 he published Flame Vine: His Voices to critical acclaim, and in 2020, Shallcross: Animal Clippers came out and won Best Books of 2020 from Kirkus Reviews again.

It is how I became a senescent old archive of American culture dancing with a cockeyed creationist on that same radio, graphomania, a writer by choice.

I didn't start writing prose until I was sixty-five. Before that, I was a songwriter. When you write song lyrics, you are squeezed a bit by the music's frame to make it work; what I love about prose is that you have this room to really expand when your whittle monster gets loose.

After living all this time, my novels are a history lesson for some and nostalgia for others. Starting to write later in life meant I had plenty of material. I have yet to experience writer's block, and my good editor keeps that whittle monster I mentioned readable.

I've started to slow down some of the more complex stuff in my recent work and just tell the story.

I have a favorite critic, James Wood, who once said, "The purer the storytelling, the better, where the purity is the embrace of sheer occurrence, unburdened by deeper human meaning."

Is writing therapeutic? I think so. I like to write in an extended hand sometimes. It is said that the motion of the cursory hand creates more serotonin in the brain. Does it? I have a sign on my wall that reads, "Don't think twice; it's all write."

www.jeyranmain.com

GOLDEN GREMLIN: A VIGOROUS PUSH FROM MISANTHROPES AND GEEZERS

Rod A. Walters

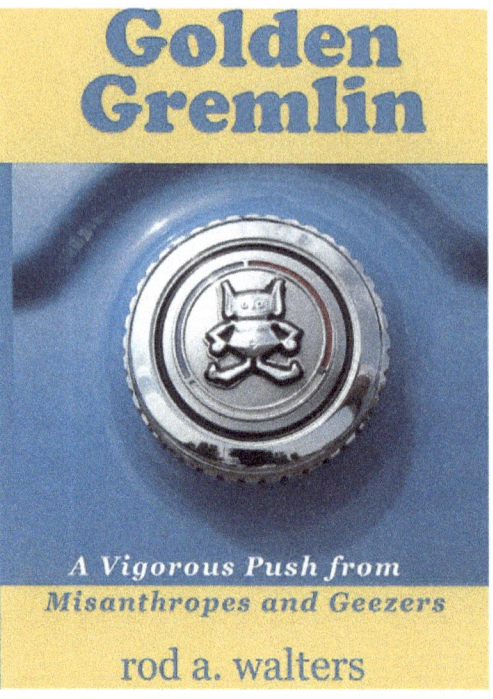

Publication Date: 2016
ISBN: 978-0-984179-20-6
Book Category/Genre: Nonfiction / Humor
Page Count: 232
Publisher: Omega Man Press

Sex sells

Written by Rod A. Walters

Of course, it does. Everybody knows that. But does it help writing? Great that you should ask because the answer is—surprise!—yes.

Some famous writer said, "When you write, you should write as if to one particular person." Great.

Confession. When that one particular person is the one to whom I am somehow attracted, then my writing tends to be more concrete, more vivid, with fewer -ly adverbs. In short, it will be written in the professional style that all these hot-shot writing consultant-speaker persons keep ranting on and on about. Why spend precious writer's $$$ on consultants when a well-chosen target person would get the same job done with a smaller hit to the old bank account?

www.jeyranmain.com

Rod A. Walters, a writing name, was a U.S. Army officer, then a corporate mechanical and chemical engineer, and now he writes. He doesn't know if he likes writing all that much, but he keeps doing it and will not stop. His pronouns are he, him, hey-you, and jackass. Currently, he lives in Rochester, New York, and keeps trying to keep pen ready, mind open, and mouth shut.

On that flowing note, another anonymous famous writer said, "Draft your stories naked."

Confession. Most of the time: NO! I couldn't stand the laughter. Some other person, not a writer, suggested instead putting a couple of mirrors in the working room, and all other persons out. Maybe.

And then, "You can think clearly only with your clothes on." (Margaret Atwood, a fabulous Canadian writer, who clearly talked nonsense this time). Why do authors have to weigh in on this topic!

Confession. For inspiration, there really are other famous-person quotes on the topic I'm drafting:

"Last night I woke up with someone squeezing my hand. It was my other hand." (William S. Burroughs, Naked Lunch).

"We hate the truth out of prudery because it is naked." (Maurice Chapelan, journalist).

"If a turtle doesn't have a shell, is he homeless or naked?" (George Carlin).

Funny, but none of these great sayings get to the point. "It's the thought that counts."

So here's the thought. When that nagging book project sits scattered around the desk, two-thirds finished, and the unfinished part needs fire in both your eyes and your pen (all right, keyboard), how to move forward? If it comes down to "Sex Sells," which of those two S-words has the more weight? Where do you have the most skin in the game? Then to whom shall ye write? Confess!!

VICTORIAN SONGLIGHT: THE BIRTHINGS OF MAGIC & MYSTERY

Kathy Martone

Publication Date: October 16, 2019
ISBN: 978-1-947381-16-2
Book Genre: Fantasy, Urban Fantasy, Paranormal, Paranormal Romance, Metaphysical Fiction
Page Count: 210
Publisher: Dreaming Big Publications

GOLD STAR CONFESSIONS

Written by Kathy Martone

Bless me, Father, for I have sinned. It has been countless years since my last confession. I confess that I ignored the writing talents I displayed at a very young age and considered myself to be without any redeeming qualities.

Growing up in a Roman Catholic family, I learned early on that women should never ever express anything positive about themselves. So, when I frequently received lavish praise from my teachers for my skills as a writer, I promptly dismissed them.

These nuns were females, were they not? Didn't they realize that it was a mortal sin for those of us born with a vagina to express and receive positive affirmations? Shaking my head in confusion and disapproval, I hid the papers with the gold stars in the upper right-hand corner, deep beneath the layers of underwear in my chest of drawers.

As the years passed, I grew more and more adept at hiding my many talents beneath the dirty underwear of my creativity, the layers soiled from multiple castigations of self-criticism, blame, and yes, even hatred. I was determined to be a good Catholic girl.

Several years ago, when I began to write my first novel, it came as quite a surprise when those sullied, self-effacing reminders simply lifted away, exposing the most delicious cache of words and thoughts. Chuckling to myself with forbidden glee, I watched and listened as the good little girl in me threw off all that dirty linen and began to play once again. To experience the resurrection of the soul, long thought dead and buried, is enriching beyond the very words I use to try and capture those long-lost gold stars.

Dr. Martone's work has been displayed in galleries in Denver, Colorado, as well as in Eureka Springs, Arkansas. In 2006 Dr. Martone self-published her first book titled, Sacred Wounds: A Love Story. Many of her short stories and essays have been published in Merge (an online literary magazine) as well as in several paperback anthologies titled Not Dead Yet 2 and Dairy Hollow Echo.

Recording those selfsame thoughts as they rush to the surface like some magnificent creature gasping for air is something I hope never to forget.

Bless me, Father, for I have sinned. I confess that I have tried to bury the writer I was meant to be. For my penance, I promise to permanently release her from her grave, never again to stifle her creativity or her thoughts.

www.jeyranmain.com

STARDUST DESTINIES I VARIATE FACING

Celinka Serre

Publication Date: May 19, 2019.
ISBN: 978-0-991996-53-7 (Digital)
ISBN: 978-0-991996-52-0 (Paperback)
Book Category/Genre: High Fantasy, Young Adult fiction, with adventure and romance subgenres.
Page Count: 452 pages
Publisher: Binky Ink (Self-published)

I Rarely Write in Consecutive Order

Written by Celinka Serre

It is so rare that I will write the story in a coherent consecutive order when writing my series. I always jump around and then put things in the proper order afterward. When I started writing Stardust Destinies 1, I started with what ended up being Chapter 9.

I have a binder full of notes in which I keep track of characters, the dates in the story, and the number of days it takes to travel from one location to another.

www.jeyranmain.com

I had to use highlighters to color code my characters and plot development notes, so I'd know which ones had to be written soon and which ones would come later. Green was for the immediate future, blue was in a bit, yellow much later, orange and pink were for later books.

Once everything that was green and blue had been written and developed, yellow became immediate, and so on. At the moment, I'm working on an installment much later in the series, and I have one group of characters in one location and another group of characters in another location.

At first, I wrote whatever ideas were fresher, and I did have a few consecutive chapters written down, but then I couldn't keep track of my story the way I wanted to anymore. So I decided to proofread what I had for the first group of characters and continue writing chapters without numbering the pages or chapters.

*elinka Serre is an indie writer *d video producer, working *eelance and having fun sharing *ntent on YouTube. She believes * the freedom of creativity and has *ver let up pursuing her dreams. *aving begun writing Stardust *estinies at the age of 19, the novel *ries is but one of her many *deavors.*

*e is also a writer of fan-fiction, *rious indie film screenplays, and *ew collaborations as well.*

Now I'm proofreading for the second group of characters, and I will write chapters for them up until the point where they meet up again with the others. Then I'll figure out which chapters go where and proceed with the rest of the book. It's a fun process, all the same, even if my ideas bounce from one time in the story to another and from one location to another. I know that once I've written what I need to, I'll be able to bring order to my creative chaos.

www.jeyranmain.com

BOOK

REVIEWS

Review Tales is proud to have completed over 1200 book reviews so far.
It is safe to say that we have seen our fair share of manuscripts. Our reviews have always been unbiased and constructive. We aim to help authors realize their strengths and encourage them to continue writing. 5 book reviews have been selected for the Spring issue.

TO APPLY FOR A BOOK REVIEW VISIT
WWW.JEYRANMAIN.COM

BRETT ATLAS

Three Things Matter Most: Linking Time, Relationships, and Money

Reviewer: Jeyran Main

Publication Date: September 2021
ISBN: 978-1-950091-54-6
Book Category/Genre: Self-help
Page Count: 219
Publisher: Addicus Books

Three Things Matter Most is a self-help book. In this book, the author asks the right questions making you ponder on what you have been doing so far in your life. 'Are you focused on what matters most?' is something I would have been asked when I was younger, but now? I wouldn't think anymore because we live in a world where we primarily run from one thing to the next.

The author embraces the impact money, time and relationships have had on us and how the three mentioned things create a meaningful life or a life with disappointment. This self-improvement book is filled with wisdom, psychology, and philosophical elements, making it rich and worth the read.

The book is divided into three parts and is organized well. It is apparent that the author has given thought and care, making sure it is not complicated or too wordy to follow.

I recommend this book to anyone who wants to learn what to focus on to make an imperative change in their life.

ANGELA PAGE AND MIA ALTIERI

There's a Dead Girl In My Yard

Reviewer: Jeyran Main

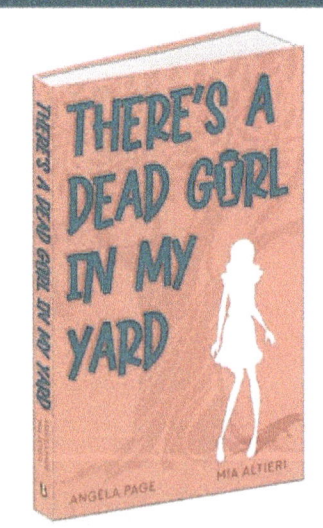

Publication Date: Dec 8, 2021
ISBN: 978-1-954396-12-8
Book Category/Genre: Crime/suspense comedy
Page Count: 304
Publisher: Barringer Publishing

There's a dead girl in my yard is a comedy crime story inspired by actual events. Poppy is a struggling actress, and her life changes when she witnesses an urn being buried. She gets involved with Dalia, a dead girl who used to be a Latina health guru.

Dalia has a lot of visitors and fans. Her fan club overwhelms Poppy, and so she begins to be like her to understand Dalia's former life as a healer and thief, and mourner manages Dalia's burial site.

I liked the story because the characters were slowly introduced, and the concept was humorous. Their personalities weren't one-dimensional or predictable. This created an interesting dynamic of a story and kept you guessing.

It was interesting to see how Dalia preferred to wear the clothes of a dead person just to bring luck for herself and life. This displayed the struggles actors face when trying to be noticed.

The comical story is thought-provoking and enjoyable to read. I recommend this book to murder mystery story readers and those who like entertaining reads.

SHALLCROSS
Charles Porter

Reviewer: Jeyran Main

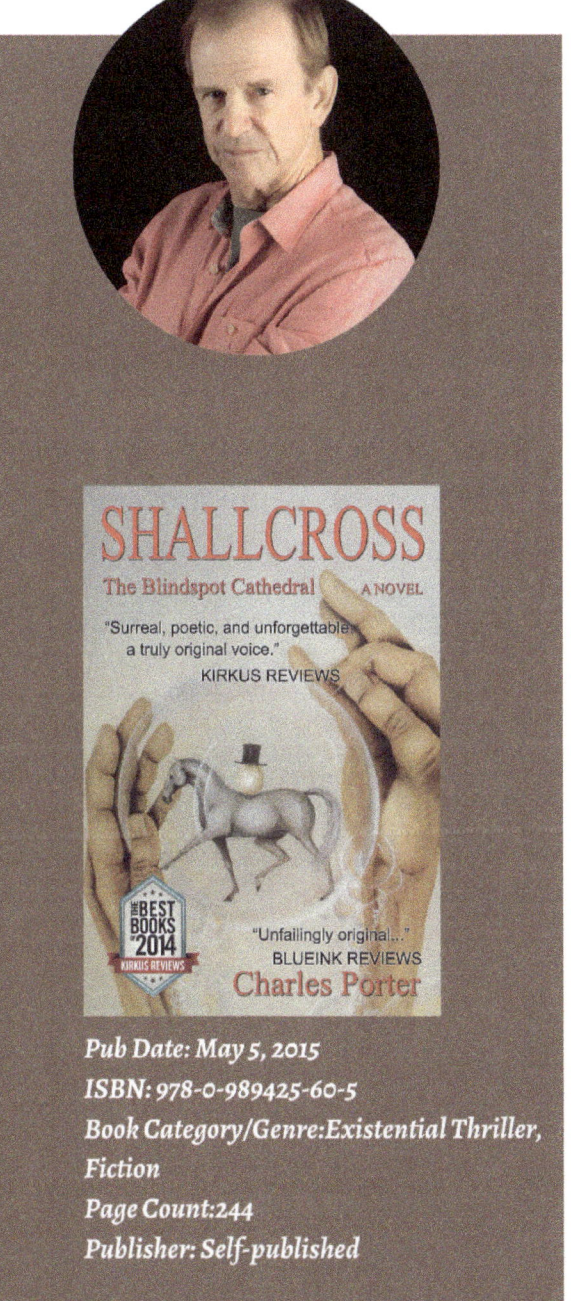

Pub Date: May 5, 2015
ISBN: 978-0-989425-60-5
Book Category/Genre: Existential Thriller, Fiction
Page Count: 244
Publisher: Self-published

Shallcross is an existential thriller fiction and a perfect tale for Halloween and horror fans. The story begins with Aubrey Shallcross and his feelings of the absence of routine since he has sold his business and is retired. Things have lost their purpose, and so he has more time on his hand to find comfort from the fear of anxiety in the familiarity of a Triple Suiter.

Things take a slight turn when we are introduced to this Triple Suiter, and you get to see how influential his mind's other voice can be. Aubrey attempts to manage and maintain his sanity by keeping himself indulged with his passions, and when he encounters love, the life he leads finds a different meaning.

The literature is dark and twisted. It has the exact kind of mystery and amusement to keep you wanting more. Aubrey's personality is indeed the catalyst for the premise, and although he has many voices in his head, he seems to still be happy.

This is a fascinating and well-written story. It is apparent how much the author has cared about creating it, and if you are a fan of this genre, you won't be disappointed.

I recommend this book to those who like to read fiction thrillers.

FISHING FOR MORE: A MEMOIR
Brett Bloemendaal

Reviewer: Jeyran Main

Pub Date: Sep 1, 2021
ISBN: 978-1-7368465-0-6 (Digital)
      978-1-7368465-1-3 (Paperback)
      978-1-7368465-2-0 (Hardcopy)
Book Category/Genre: Memoir
Page Count: 238
Publisher: Self-published

Fishing for more is a non-fiction memoir about Brett and how he reshapes his life after losing his grandfather. As Brett's psychological state deteriorates, he re-lives the lasting memories with his father and how much he loved their fishing trips.

Brett buys a boat and begins reacquainting himself with fishing and what owning a boat entails. He enjoys his moments with his dad so much that the thought comes into his mind, what if he did this for a living?

The literature is written with such emotion and delightfully added humor that it is hard to think of anything else but continue reading. The narration is honest and is filled with descriptive notions of Brett's thoughts. I appreciated how much love he had for his father and how much value Brett placed on the time they had left together.

It isn't easy to make a memoir this enjoyable to read. I recommend this book to those who love a good father-son story and like fishing stories.

BELOW TORRENTIAL HILL
Jonathan Koven

Reviewer: Jeyran Main

Publication Date: March 2021
ISBN: 979-8-488308-80-0
Book Category/Genre: Literary Fiction / Coming-of-age / Magical Realism
Page Count: 190
Publisher: Electric Eclectic (winner of the 2020 Electric Eclectic Novella Prize)

Below Torrential Hill is a coming-of-age magical realism story. The book is mainly about Tristan and his troubled life dealing with his mom, young love, relationships with his family, and a magical comet passing by. Tristan is a loner and doesn't really trust people. He lost his father a long time ago, and the stem of his death still follows him at 16. When his stepfather leaves, Tristen is left with his Mom, Lucy, who doesn't treat him well.

Tristan is not only taking care of himself but also has to watch over Lucy too. At Christmas time, Lucy claims to be hearing and noticing strange things; Tristan isn't sure what to believe.

What I particularly enjoyed about the story was that underneath all the paranormal occurrences, all the elements that were sprinkled within the pages, and all the heartwarming messages, you could not help but learn a few things about yourself or at least remember how things were when you were young.

There is a certain thrill in the literature that keeps you wanting more. The author has written an incredible story. I appreciate the balance between real-life struggles and the magical side of things. Tristan was such a relatable character in so many ways and managed to highlight the key elements of the story.

I recommend this book to those who like to read captivating stories full of hope.

Words of Wisdom

Contributors:
VK Tritschler
Kaleb Quist
Michael J. Brooks
Maxwell F. Hurley
Donald Furrow-Scott

"BELIEVE AND ACT AS IF IT WERE IMPOSSIBLE TO FAIL." – CHARLES KETTERING

WWW.JEYRANMAIN.COM

A TOWN CALLED NOWHERE

VK Tritschler

Good Enough

WRITTEN BY VK TRITSCHLER

When I moved to Australia and started writing books, I joined the local writing group. I remember very clearly the first time I walked into that room full of authors, poets, playwrights, and other writers. The tremble of my hands as I typed the first sentences on the screen after getting a writing prompt. I felt unaccomplished in comparison. Their long lists of books and stories, and their understanding of the craft were inspiring, but intimidating.

But something, which I had hoped for but still felt unexpected, eventually happened. I started to absorb the knowledge. I picked up new skills, made new friends, and as the days turned into weeks, and then to years; I found my craft blossom under their careful gaze. My writing became clearer and brighter. The form took shape and the ideas from my mind began to develop on the page. Soon I had finished one book. Then another. And still, I kept going.

But that shaking never left me. The feeling that I was still somehow not enough to be called an author yet. And I wondered if I ever would.

Then one day, I got to meet and spend time with someone I would consider a famous author. Bestselling worldwide, professional, and with years of experience, the tremble was back. But he smiled and introduced himself so calmly and casually. Before I knew it, I had forgotten that he even was famous. We chatted openly about the successes and failures of writing. The common challenges that all writers seem to face from time to time. It was reassuring to hear that he still had those moments too. And then he uttered the words that gave me a moment's pause.

'Sometimes I feel like my work just isn't good enough.'

It was then that I realized something. Being an author isn't an end game. It doesn't have a clearly defined line which after you have passed it you have reached the end. There is no end to this chase. The elusive chase to achieve and write better, bolder, stronger. You get attached to and lose characters along the way. You build and destroy plotlines and universes. But nothing removes that feeling you get when your next book is complete. I will never be rich enough, famous enough, or have written enough to ever remove that feeling. To turn the pages and feel the sheen of the paper under your touch. Your worlds and thoughts are laid out and exposed for the world to read. That is both thrilling and terrifying.

So, I continue to have a shaky hand whenever I start a new story. And as much as I love to read feedback from my readership, I am always cautious to remind myself that I am an author. My words mean something, even if they aren't destined to be in the writing hall of fame. But to write is to create. And that desire will drive me onward.

Publication Date: April 22, 2021
ISBN: 064-8-383-53-9
Book Category/Genre: Paranormal Romance
Page Count: 198
Publisher: Praelectus Publishing

THE GOLDEN AGE

Kaleb Quist

The Golden Age of Oversaturation

WRITTEN BY KALEB QUIST

If you're reading this, that means you've been born at the best time in human history for creativity. Thanks to the internet, you have access to all the world's music, literature, and films, right at your fingertips. Likewise, you have the power to share your art with anyone in the world, at any given time.
But of course, every revolution has its problems, and the internet revolution is no exception.

When I published my novel "The Golden Age," I quickly realized that I'm nothing more than a fish in a sea of aspiring writers… And a small fish, at that.

The publishing industry has become a vacuum, where countless voices are lost among the endless void of space. It makes me wonder how many Hemingway's and Fitzgerald's will never be discovered, simply because they never had their chance to shine.

We owe artists a great debt for giving us the gift of escapism in a harrowing world, which often needs escaping. Despite this, artists are rarely given their due.

One might think this diminishes the value of an artist. But in our world today, it actually makes them even more valuable.

Artists know they might never be discovered, and yet they'll fight through hell just to make themselves heard. Forever burning with an earnest desire to share their work with other people, so they can enjoy it with them.

Every artist's work is special simply because they created it using their own thoughts, dreams, and experiences. In the end, nobody can speak your voice for you. The discipline in forging art is valued higher than the stars since they will never have the power to create as you do.

The market may seem oversaturated, but now is the most important time in history to be creative. Self-expression is equivalent to godliness since it brings us closer to an all-creative God.

So go ahead, write that song. Make that movie. Write for writing's sake. Creativity isn't a privilege, but an obligation.

If you're happy with what you're doing, then you're already a success in your own right.

Publication Date: October 23, 2021
ISBN: 979-8-540492-66-9
Book Category/Genre: Humor, Slice-of-Life, Literary Fiction
Page Count: 311
Publisher: Self-Published

REPUBLIC FALLING: ADVENT OF A NEW DAWN

Michael J. Brooks

Lessons Learned from the Bumps, Bruises, and Trials of Publishing

WRITTEN BY MICHAEL J. BROOKS

When I launched into my journey as a fiction author, one of my biggest hurdles to overcome was that my prose was stiff, way too formal. And that was because I was accustomed to academic writing, but the strict standards for academic writing don't apply to creative writing. By "standards," I'm not referring to punctuation and grammar; those should always be on point. When you write creatively, allow yourself to loosen up and have fun with your prose. Character dialogue doesn't have to sound formal. In reality, people use slang; people may have nicknames for friends, people use words like "kinda, gonna, ain't, shoulda." But not only can character dialogue be informal, but the narration can also be informal. Have fun with your prose!

Editing can be tough, no matter how good a writer you are. I hired editors for my first two novels, Exodus Conflict and Exodus Conflict: New Genesis. Since I've grown as a writer and have become pretty adept at spotting punctuation, grammar, and plot errors, I didn't hire an editor for Republic Falling: Advent of a New Dawn; I received positive reviews and critiques from Readers' Favorite and the BookLife Prize. But let me tell you, it cost me more time and money by not employing the skills of an editor. There were times I thought I had everything squared away, only to discover a punctuation or grammar mistake here and there or a discrepancy in the plot.

Then I would feel certain I had caught all errors, only to find more when I read over my work again. So multiple times, I had to re-upload my novel to Amazon, Barnes & Noble, and Ingram Spark; and with Ingram Spark, there's a fee to upload your book every time you want to make changes to it. Also, I wonder how an editor would've further polished and contribute to my story. It's beneficial to have a second pair of eyes on your work. So, definitely hire an editor, or if you have a friend with exceptional editing skills, hire them. And don't worry, Republic Falling: Advent of a New Dawn is error-free after much hard work.

I believe that book competitions are fantastic. Many allow you to submit your novel before it's published. Placing in such a competition gives you a credit you can use for book promotion pre-release. And some competitions, such as the BookLife Prize, will write you a critique even if you don't place, which you can also use for promotion. In terms of reviews for Amazon, Amazon doesn't permit an author to pay for reviews. You can distribute free copies with the hope of a free review. I don't believe in paying for reviews. My philosophy is that it already cost me a lot of time and money to produce the novel, so why should I pay someone to use/read a product created at my own expense that I'm providing for free? However, everyone's philosophy is different, and I respect theirs. You can pay for promotion, which is not the same as paying for a review.

I say, before paying anyone for any type of service, search for bloggers who accept free copies for the possibility of a free review, hence the word "possibility." Reedsy has a good list of such bloggers, which I have utilized, and some of those bloggers host author interviews and book tours. Another way to get reviews is to use NetGalley. Major publishers, as well as self-published authors, use NetGalley to obtain reviews pre-release. Yes, NetGalley costs to list a novel, more for self-published authors; but in my opinion, using NetGalley is better than paying multiple reviewers. I have just discovered NetGalley, and I wish I had known about the website before publishing Republic Falling: Advent of a New Dawn.

Lastly, I'd like to say that there are several billion people in the world, and not everyone is going to love your work, just like you don't love every author's work. So, don't get discouraged by a few less-than-stellar reviews of your novel. I hope this article may be helpful to any author, traditional or self-published.

Publication date: October 12, 2021
ISBN: 978-1-737929-30-7
Genre: Science Fiction
Page count: 358 pages
Publisher: Independently Published

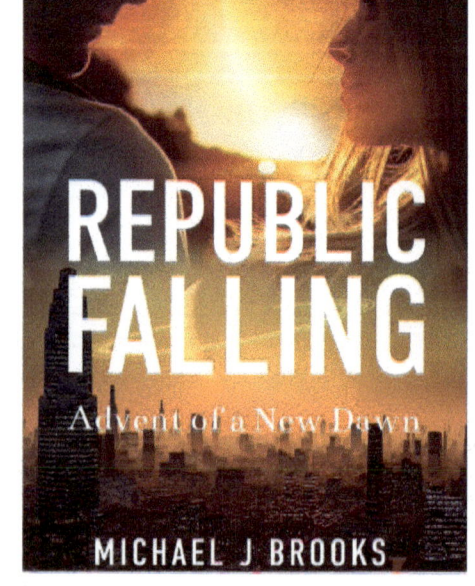

LIT, PART I: THE DARK IGNITES

Maxwell F. Hurley

It's Not a Good Fit for Us

MAXWELL F. HURLEY

Writing is pleasurable torture, isn't it? You've expended the prized time that you hold dear and written your story, a reflection of your soul, a piece of yourself embedded within. The time has come, and you take the bravest step, you shop for a publisher. With high hopes of holding the next great novel of your generation, you get your first response. "It's just not a good fit for us."

Rejection! It stings, doesn't it? Those denial letters are a direct shot into the gut with a slow bleed if you're anything like me. Who knew a faceless stranger casting off the hours of your work could be truly devastating? Through perseverance with determination and perhaps a little grace of God, the story is published. Your book is now on the shelves.

You are on cloud nine. Perhaps, the colors outside are a bit brighter. Then, you hear a pop, and the dirt from the ground gets into your mouth upon impact. Marketing your book becomes a harsh reality. The book market is flooded, and you're not wearing a life jacket. The ease of self-publishing books has brought an abundance of authors, just like yourself, with hopes of getting their unique stories out to the masses. Franchise bookstores won't shelve your book. Most locally-owned stores take new author books on consignment, but no one knows what talent you have shared. When you realize that readers aren't purchasing your book, it may take you down a spiral of cynicism.

Cast out all your self-doubt! You accomplished something extraordinary. You took that brave step to put yourself out there for others to judge others, good or bad. Remember, it's just their opinion. Take in constructive criticism; try to see where they are coming from. Perhaps it's something you could incorporate. Your writing is only going to get better with each completed sentence. You have something special in you that needs to be brought to the world. There's someone for every story.

Publish Date: 2021
ISBN: 978-1- 78695 5-84-5
Book Category/Genre: YA Fantasy (Modern Day)
Page Count: 312
Publisher: Double Dragon

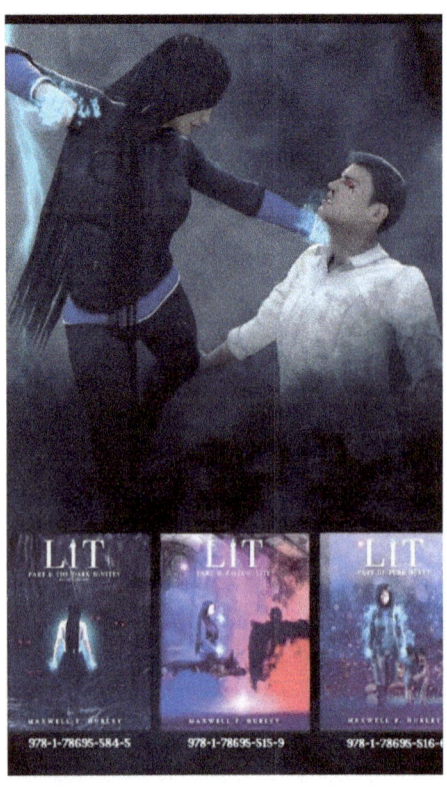

IMMORTALIZE

Donald Furrow-Scott

Whom are You Writing For?

DONALD FURROW-SCOTT

Watercolors and oils. Chords and harmony. Rhyme and meter. In clay, wood, stone, or gold, the artist crafts their imagination into being with a summoning to rival the creation of the earth and heavens. In so many ancient legends, the gods built our universe and then got lonely for someone to share it with.

You feel compelled to write. For whom?

I don't mean your target audience. Publisher Rocket can help your writing business with that audience far better than any advice from me. I'm speaking of your writing spirit.

For almost twenty years, our winery has hosted musicians and bands on Saturday nights. We've heard some damn good musicians and a lot of effort from those trying to be. So many of them want to be on the radio. Yet, the first hour was all we needed to know. Those that failed were not invited back. Those that weren't quite there might get invited back again. Those bands, whom people came in asking 'who is that?' and talking about how good there were, got invited back again and again.

All of those bands played for random visitors on a Saturday night. A crapshoot of weather, food, wine, and moonlight all in a lucky culmination, to be certain. But who exactly heard the hours of practice that made the musicians who they were? When my writing was in its infancy in the 1980s, I'd plan stories for weeks, practicing, and then cast my spell upon a group of a half-dozen players over a long evening.

I was in heaven. I shaped adventure stories that friends talked about for months, even years. Some even forty years later remember them with a fondness as if they had seen a great movie. It fulfilled my artist's needs to express and share, yet I was only writing for a few friends.

My stories grew and expanded upon each other, lengthening into long weekends over two decades, forming a foundational series for only four players. There were long, elaborate plots filled with mystical allies and confounding, evil arch-nemesis.

As the age for computer forums began, the exchange mutated. Now, games lasted months and years, with breaks as long as the next upload. New players perused the thread works and lurked in the forum shadows, ready to join in if the right chords of their interest were struck. Not unlike a band on a Saturday night, whose tunes drifting on the air might entice someone passing by to stay and listen longer.

Some writers say the characters in their stories speak to them. My wife was both floored and enlightened to discover that, during the movie "The Man Who Invented Christmas,' she asked myself and our daughter, who's also a writer, 'if our characters were like Dicken's, following him around in his day.' We both laughed and expressed how true it was. Show that movie to any loved one who doesn't understand you as a writer. Still, other authors say their characters speak through them That these characters tell their stories, with the writer only acting as the channeling medium. One wonders if the writer was not there, would the ghostly character have sought out another writer to tell their tale through?

You may write for a lonely spirit, a teacher, a publisher, a raving fan base, or a friend. But you keep writing because practice makes perfect, or so they say.

I have written and self-published novels. I have poured every ounce of energy into pages as if I was some literary symphony conductor entertaining a mute audience. I have never achieved popularity. I do not know the heady feeling of best-sellers and the accolades of industry accomplishment. My writing makes more bills than it pays. Yet, if even one person connected with my story, that imaginary character was heard. I am happy to have been the medium.

You see, you write for you.

Everything else is luck, business, distraction, and circumstance.

Find yourself in the practice of your art.

Publication Date: January, 2020
ISBN: 173389196X
Book Category/Genre: Ancient History Fiction
Page Count: 345
Publisher: Sahhaar Publishing LLC

Author Interview

Contributors:
Tosca Lee
Susanna Allen
Jennifer Allis Provost
Mercedes R. Lackey

TOSCA LEE

About Me

Tosca Lee is the New York Times bestselling author of eleven novels including The Line Between, The Progeny, The Legend of Sheba, and Iscariot. Her work has been translated into seventeen languages and optioned for TV and film.

The Line Between

When did you first realize you wanted to be a writer?

It took me a while! I always loved writing growing up and had even won several contests as a young person, but I'd wanted to be a ballerina since I was a toddler. Growing up, that was my #1 goal in life. I danced semi-professionally as a teenager and spent my summers away from home dancing. After an injury, I realized this dream of professional ballet might not happen. During my freshman year at college, I reassessed my relationship with writing. I'd loved reading all my life, and for the first time, I wondered if I could provide readers with a fantastic escape the way, so many authors had for me.

What would you say is your interesting writing quirk?

I write best at night. Though it gets harder and harder the older I get! I also have to have my favorite snacks while working—buttered movie popcorn is one of my favorites, which is extremely messy and difficult to eat if you're trying to type.

Is there anything you would like to confess about as an author?

I dread first drafts. I fear them. And then I get in there and have fun. But I love shaping the first draft into a second, third, and final draft (how many iterations later that might come).

As a child, what did you want to do when you grew up?

A ballerina for sure

What would you say is your interesting writing quirk?

I write best at night. Though it gets harder and harder the older I get! I also have to have my favorite snacks while working—buttered movie popcorn is one of my favorites, which is extremely messy and difficult to eat if you're trying to type.

How did you get your book published?

My very first novel wasn't published. I tried and got soundly rejected by a major New York agency. The blessing is that the letter pointed out why they rejected it, which became a learning syllabus for me. My second novel—a project of nine long years—is one I never finished. My third novel is the one that became my first published book. I wrote it in six weeks, and it took six years before my new agent, and I found a home for it. That was 2006. Since then, I've published 10 more, and my next releases spring 2023.

What do you like to do when you're not writing?

Sleep. Eat. Clean out the fridge, closets, and drawers. I really love cleaning things out.

Publication Date: January 29, 2019
ISBN: 1501169092
Book Category/Genre: Medical thriller, suspense
Page Count: 384
Publisher: Howard Books/Simon & Schuster

About Me

Susan Conley, she is the author of Drama Queen and The Fidelity Project, both published by Headline UK; Many Brave Fools: A Story of Addiction, Dysfunction, Codependency...and Horses is available from Trafalgar Square Books. Susanna is living her life by the three Rs—reading, writing, and horseback riding—and can generally be found on her sofa with her e-reader, gazing out a window and thinking about made-up people or cantering around in circles. She loves every minute of it.

SUSANNA ALLEN
That Magic Mischief

When did you first realize you wanted to be a writer?

It took me a while! I always loved writing growing up and had even won several contests as a young person, but I'd wanted to be a ballerina since I was a toddler. Growing up, that was my #1 goal in life. I danced semi-professionally as a teenager and spent my summers away from home dancing. After an injury, I realized this dream of professional ballet might not happen. During my freshman year at college, I reassessed my relationship with writing. I'd loved reading all my life, and for the first time, I wondered if I could provide readers with a fantastic escape the way, so many authors had for me.

What would you say is your interesting writing quirk?

I write best at night. Though it gets harder and harder the older I get! I also have to have my favorite snacks while working—buttered movie popcorn is one of my favorites, which is extremely messy and difficult to eat if you're trying to type.

Is there anything you would like to confess about as an author?

I dread first drafts. I fear them. And then I get in there and have fun. But I love shaping the first draft into a second, third, and final draft (how many iterations later that might come).

As a child, what did you want to do when you grew up?

A ballerina for sure

What would you say is your interesting writing quirk?

I write best at night. Though it gets harder and harder the older I get! I also have to have my favorite snacks while working—buttered movie popcorn is one of my favorites, which is extremely messy and difficult to eat if you're trying to type.

How did you get your book published?

My very first novel wasn't published. I tried and got soundly rejected by a major New York agency. The blessing is that the letter pointed out why they rejected it, which became a learning syllabus for me. My second novel—a project of nine long years—is one I never finished. My third novel is the one that became my first published book. I wrote it in six weeks, and it took six years before my new agent, and I found a home for it. That was 2006. Since then, I've published 10 more, and my next releases spring 2023.

What do you like to do when you're not writing?

Sleep. Eat. Clean out the fridge, closets, and drawers. I really love cleaning things out.

Pub Date: October 1, 2021
ISBN 10: 195-3-290-12-4
ISBN 13: 978-1-953290-12-0
Book Category/Genre: Contemporary Paranormal Romance
Page Count: 306
Publisher: Ally Press

About Me

Jennifer Allis Provost writes books about faeries, orcs, elves, and zombies. She grew up in the wilds of Western Massachusetts and had read every book in the local library by age twelve. (It was a small library.) An early love of mythology and folklore led to her epic fantasy series, The Chronicles of Parthalan, and her day job as a cubicle monkey helped shape her urban fantasy, Copper Girl. She's working on her MFA in Creative Nonfiction when she's not writing about things that go bump in the night (and sometimes during the day).

JENNIFER ALLIS PROVOST

Oleander

Where did you get your information or idea for your book?

My idea for Oleander came from an open call for an anthology. The call was for a short story themed on final decisions. It definitely had nothing to do with poisons, witches, or seers! But I started writing, and my main character, Eli, told me exactly who she was and which this story would go. Needless to say, I never ended up submitting to that anthology, but that story became Oleander, the first book in the Poison Garden series.

What was one of the most surprising things you learned in creating your book?

The main character in Oleander, Eli Moore, is a seer who sometimes uses poisons to talk to the dead. Naturally, I started researching poisons and was shocked to learn how many standard garden and house plants are poisonous. Read those little nursery tags before you bring them home, people!

Make a confession about being an author.

Writing for a living isn't easy, and it definitely isn't glamourous, but I rather do this than anything else in the world.

What do you like to do when you're not writing?

I garden, bake (okay, I binge the Great British Bake Off and eat Oreos), and make crafts and custom book swag.

When did you first realize you wanted to be a writer?

I've always made up stories, and I started writing them down sometime in middle school. Around 2007-2008 I realized that I really wanted to publish them, not just hoard the stories for myself. Seventeen books later, here we are.

How did you get your book published?

My very first novel wasn't published. I tried and got soundly rejected by a major New York agency. The blessing is that the letter pointed out why they rejected it, which became a learning syllabus for me. My second novel—a project of nine long years—is one I never finished. My third novel is the one that became my first published book. I wrote it in six weeks, and it took six years before my new agent, and I found a home for it. That was 2006. Since then, I've published 10 more, and my next releases spring 2023.

Publication Date: 06/14/2022
ISBN: 979-8-9856750-0-9
Book Category/Genre: Urban Fantasy
Page Count: 300
Publisher: Bellatrix Press

About Me

Mercedes Lackey has written and published 142 books in many series, including The Secret World Chronicles, Hunter, Valdemar, Elemental Masters, SERRAted Edge, Elvenbane, and Obsidian Mountain series from Hyperion, DAW, Baen, Tor, and many others.

MERCEDES R. LACKEY

The Silver Bullets of Annie Oakley

When did you first realize you wanted to be a writer?

Probably about the time I first was able to read stories for myself; I was writing for school "literary magazines" by about the seventh grade. I kept it up through high school and in college, and after I graduated from college, I discovered science fiction fandom and fanzines, and I began writing for those. I got a lot of practice doing those fanzine stories!

Where did you get your information or idea for your book?

This is part of my Elemental Masters series, featuring magic during the Edwardian Era. I actually purloined the title (The Silver Bullets of Annie Oakley) from a list of gaming scenarios a tabletop gaming writer I know (Owen K. Stephenson) was toying with for a homebrew game he was going to run. The title kind of tells it all!

What would you say is your interesting writing quirk?

I have twelve parrots, and most of them get out-of-cage time with me, so I generally write with a parrot on the back of my chair.

Is there anything you would like to confess about as an author?

I wish the books I've done and like the best were the ones the readership liked best as well! Ah well.

As a child, what did you want to do when you grew up?

Marine biologist. I'm kind of glad now I didn't go into it; I'd be bald from tearing my hair out over the state of the oceans.

What was one of the most surprising things you learned in creating your book?

Frank Butler, Annie's husband, was a man so far ahead of his time that it still astonishes me. He was just as good (or nearly) a marksman as she was, but he seems to have had no trouble with the notion of taking a back seat to her and putting her promotion first. He must have been very secure in his self-worth, never to have shown a second of unhappiness at being the second-fiddle in the partnership.

Is there anything you would like to confess about as an author?

What do you like to do when you're not writing?

I costume dolls (they don't object when you stick pins in them) as some of my book characters, make jewelry of many sorts, and I do just about every form of needlework there is. I'm particularly taken with needle-felting at the moment; very therapeutic when you want to stab something a million times.

Publication Date: Jan 11, 2022
ISBN: ISBN-10 : 075641217X
ISBN-13 : 978-0-756412-17-3
Book Category/Genre: Fantasy/Historical Fantasy
Page Count: 288
Publisher: DAW Books

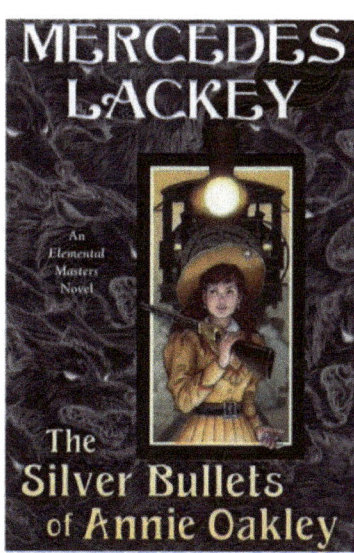

About Me

Neil attributes his love of the writing process to his formative education at the Green Meadow Waldorf School, where he understood that classes such as music, dance, and theater, writing, literature, legends, and myths, were not simply subjected to be learned, but lessons to be experienced.

NEIL PERRY GORDON

Otzi's Odyssey

When did you first realize you wanted to be a writer?

Five years ago, after a lifetime searching for a creative mode of expression, I discovered fiction writing in which I had some skills. Since then, my passion has carried me forward with eight novels and another one in the works.

What would you say is your interesting writing quirk?

I write short chapters consisting of, on average, four to five pages each. This had become not only a quirk but also a featured style of my books that readers seem to have enjoyed.

How do you schedule your life when you're writing?

I write when I'm able to isolate myself from distractions, though my ideas have no restrictions as they seem to flow throughout the day, inspired by my surroundings.

Where did you get your information or ideas for your book?

I like to select a stimulating situation within a historical context then develop an adventure story around the event. I then commit myself to research, looking for celebrated individuals and weaving them into my novel.

What was one of the most surprising things you learned in creating your book?

In Otzi's Odyssey, a novel examining the metaphysical, I realized my writing had become my spiritual practice.

Pub Date: November 25, 2021
ISBN: 978-1732667-73-0
Book Category/Genre: Metaphysical Fiction
Page Count: 353
Publisher: Self-published

Starred Books

What does it mean to be lonely? So much more than isolation, as these stories explain through gritty characters slogging through the human experience. Albert Camus said there is only one serious philosophical question or problem: Deciding whether life is worth living. How To Be Lonely tries in small part to show that no matter how hard or inane life can be, perhaps there can be a sliver of hope found, but that will entail that we either ignore the difficult realities the world presents or open our minds and accept that the rotten parts exist with the beneficent.

Pub Date: 3/17/21
ISBN 10: 173-2-027-57-9
ISBN-13: 978-1-732027-57-2
Book Category/Genre: Literary Fiction/ Short Stories
Page Count: 226 pages
Publisher: WSC Press

"The Search For Synergy" is the first book in The Talisman Series by author Brett Salter. It follows the exploits of two middle-school boys, Rome Lockheed and Julian Rider, as they transition from normal kids into epic warriors fighting for the existence of the Earth realm. Rome is secretly a fire dragon from the Den of Volcana placed under a spell that hides his true form. Julian is an oddball, up-and-coming knight with a case of the "try-hards." Together, they perform an ancient pact that bonds their lives and souls forever. Under the tutelage and guidance of an eccentric, local librarian, Mr. Jones, the two learn of an impending invasion from an archaic evil desperate to invade from the other side of The Void.

Publication Date: May 31, 2017
ISBN: 978-1-542914-84-0
Book Category/Genre: MG/YA Fantasy
Page Count: 220
Publisher: Kindle Direct

Starred Books

In 2120, New America is the world leader in technology and individual freedom. Why, then, has seventeen-year-old Fae Luna felt like an isolated prisoner her entire life?

She survived the worst of the foster care system by honing her skills as a top-level hacker and thanks to the support of her humanoid robot, Sunny, who is illegally upgraded to a human-level AI.

Will Fae choose the enhancement or trust her own exceptional mind to defeat a secretive and powerful force threatening all New Americans?

Publication Date: 3/24/2021
ISBN: 1736745115
Book Category/Genre: Sci-fi Mystery/Adventure
Page Count: 413
Publisher: Sunset Over Peconic Books

Naiche Decker is engaged! And no one is more surprised by it than her. But first, she has one more mission. The Lovelace is ordered to respond to a distress call from unexplored space and from a crew whom all died 200 years ago. What they find is not only amazing but potentially lethal. If Lt. Decker is going to make it down the aisle, she will have to survive the dangers of planet Tolu first.

Publication Date: March 16, 2021
ISBN: 1941072895
Book Category/Genre: Science Fiction
Page Count: 236
Publisher: D. X. Varos, Ltd.

Starred Books

You are special

Kristian Hägglund

Publication Date: Jan 10, 2022
ISBN: 978-9-152709-59-7
Book Category/Genre: Picturebook
Page Count: 26
Publisher: Kristian Hägglund

You do know that you are very, very special, right?

You are special is a poetic little children's book about the uniqueness of each human being and the unwavering value of each individual. The book aims to strengthen and inspire the reader by lifting otherwise elusive topics around self-esteem and self-worth simply and playfully.

Perfect as a gift to a loved one! It could also serve as a springboard for the parent or teacher who wants to open up for deeper conversations with the children.

www.ingramcontent.com/pod-product-compliance
Lightning Source LLC
Chambersburg PA
CBHW061105070526
44579CB00011B/146